The Dust Settles

The Dust Settles
Grieving through Poetry and Prose

Gina Mingoia

LIGHTNING TOWER PRESS

The Dust Settles by Gina Mingoia

Published by Lightning Tower Press, LLC
P.O. Box 381
Shoreham, NY 11786

Copyright © 2022 Gina Elizabeth Mingoia

All rights reserved. No portion of this book may be reproduced in any form without permission from the publisher, except as permitted by U.S. copyright law. For permissions, address Lightning Tower Press, LLC.
lightningtowerpress@gmail.com

Cover design by Jacqueline Mingoia

ISBN 979-8-9865558-9-8 (Print)

ISBN 979-8-9865558-8-1 (Ebook)

Printed in the United States.

First Edition: 2022

10 9 8 7 6 5 4 3 2

The Dust Settles

Grieving through Poetry and Prose

Gina Mingoia

LIGHTNING TOWER PRESS

The Dust Settles by Gina Mingoia

Published by Lightning Tower Press, LLC
P.O. Box 381
Shoreham, NY 11786

Copyright © 2022 Gina Elizabeth Mingoia

All rights reserved. No portion of this book may be reproduced in any form without permission from the publisher, except as permitted by U.S. copyright law. For permissions, address Lightning Tower Press, LLC.
lightningtowerpress@gmail.com

Cover design by Jacqueline Mingoia

ISBN 979-8-9865558-9-8 (Print)

ISBN 979-8-9865558-8-1 (Ebook)

Printed in the United States.

First Edition: 2022

10 9 8 7 6 5 4 3 2

With love for Salvatore Mingoia, the best dad I ever had.

Contents

the beginning 3
the middle 31
the healing 69
Resources 95
Author's Note 99
Acknowledgements 101

I answer the heroic question, "Death, where is thy sting?" with "It is here in my heart and mind and memories."

Maya Angelou, *Wouldn't Take Nothing from My Journey Now*

1

sand dirt dust

whipping in the wind

skin rubbed raw

ears clogged

eyes burning

pelted with particles

hair pulling knotting sticking

can't speak

can't think

can't breathe

disoriented

this is the beginning

I have discovered that time travel exists.
I have hurtled through time, against my will.
Surely, that is the only explanation.
For I have aged disproportionately
and now I am alone.
My friends have not changed
my friends have not aged
but I have lived several decades
in the course of just one day,
and now I am all alone.

The Dust Settles

I should've taken the time to see what it's worth,

because here we are:

at the end of all the angels left on Earth;

at the end of the 8:30 text

pancakes are done!

and *oops—ate them all!* by 8:31;

at the end of *I changed your strings*

at the end of *I tickle your feet*

at the end of daddy-daughter days

at the end of *Dad is great—!*

at the end of stability, reliability, safety, peace

at the end

at the end of all the angels left on Earth.

if money could've paid you off
I'd've sold everything that I own
if time could've held you at bay long enough
I'd've stopped every clock on this Earth
if misery alone could've satisfied you
I'd've taken an oath of despair
if blood could've quenched your thirst for death
I'd've torn my own heart from my chest

but you don't care about the big shot doctors
or the stem cells imported from Europe
you don't care about experimental treatments
or the hopes and the wishes and prayers
you didn't care he was in the best city
the world's greatest doctors by his bed
you didn't care that he was so deeply loved—
didn't care he was my dad

The Dust Settles

You looked me in the eye
just hold on a little longer
it'll be alright
You stood right next to me
the sun is coming, little darling—
I know you didn't mean to lie.

The leaves that fall from our tree
that leave whole branches bare
are beaten by weather, crushed underfoot
until they are crumbled and sprinkled into the air—
and I think the same is happening, too,
inside my aching, empty chest:

ashes to ashes, dust to dust.

The hospital is a half hour drive from my house.
Half an hour there, half an hour back.
Every day.
Sometimes twice a day.
I spent every drive praying
desperately
if God needed to take my father
he would take me first
so I wouldn't have to see a world without my dad.
God didn't listen to me.
And I hope it is because there is some
greater purpose for me in this world.
But I can't help but think it is because
God simply does not like me.

I reorganized the living room the night before to make room for a hospice bed, and I was sitting on the misplaced couch when my mom called / my dad's bosses came up to the door to get us / the window was open just a crack, but it was raining and we were on the expressway and the water was streaming down the car and in my window and I was getting soaked / a woman just off the bridge in the city gave us the middle finger because we were in a police car / my dad's bosses walked us in and up the elevator and pushed the elevator buttons for us / my mom greeted us as the elevator doors opened / Karen and Veronica each took one of my arms as we left the hospital room / I stood outside the hospital, not knowing who to stand next to / my dad was not there.

The Dust Settles

I'm not on fire but I'm
surrounded by flames,
licking and lapping and
charring the ground
around me.
And the heat courses up my body from my feet,
tearing through my stomach
up, but not out,
boiling the blood in my chest,
burning my throat,
stinging my eyes.

I'm not on fire but I'm
surrounded.
And to get out of this ring is to burn—
badly and deeply,
profoundly.
But to stay inside it is to burn—
slowly.
from the outside in.
from my feet up.
to drown in my own boiling blood.

I have a dead dad— And as soon as I say that, everyone knows: to have a dead dad is a very, very bad thing. They say sorry. I know: to have a dead dad is a very, very bad thing. I'm sad. All the time. Because to have a dead dad is, of course, a very, very bad thing. But once in a while, when I remember something—when I see a video, hear his voice, reread his texts—I am hit by the magnitude of the loss. To have a dead dad is an abstract idea. A very, very, bad thing, yes. Sad, yes. And abstracted. But the death of my dad, that one specific human being, who made guitar tutorials for YouTube and ended them with *call me if you have any questions!*, who made peanut butter and jelly on Ritz crackers for my sister's friends when they went through high school breakups, who watched the same documentary for a week because he kept falling asleep and rewatching the same ten minutes, who called me on my lunch break to eat lunch with me ten miles away, who drove twenty miles per hour because he didn't feel like pressing the gas, who ate cereal from a plastic cup with his tongue, who stretched before and after every run, who did headstands in the kitchen, who built my sister a pushup counter, who glued my princess tea set back together (almost every week), who laughed and cared and loved—

That's devastating.

You cover your face with your hands,
and she thinks you're really gone.
She has yet to learn

permanence

But she'll turn fourteen, or fifteen,
her grandmother will freeze,
and her grandfather will forget,
and her friend will hit his head,
and her father will promise it won't get worse
and then it will
and then she'll see she was right from the start—
humans, loved ones, are, in fact,

impermanent

She knows:

What's gone is dead

and what's dead is gone.

But that doesn't mean life goes on.

I hated myself for wasting time
at home instead of with my friends
I hated him for leaving,
as if he chose to hit his head
I loathed every piece and part of me
that trusted I had time

I vowed that I would make a change:
spend more time out with friends
And now here I stand, three years elapsed,
wishing I hadn't changed

I hate myself for wasting time out
when I should've stayed home, stayed in
I can't hate him for leaving—
I should've known this is how cancer ends.
And now I don't know where to run,
who to love, and how to choose.
Whomever I choose, I am doomed to regret
all my time wasted at the next time of death
Who will it be?
And with whom should I spend the rest of this butchered eternity?
I hit my knees and I hope and I pray that
nobody is lost before me.

She spent her whole life collecting teacups.
She lined them all up on her shelf.
Teacups and saucers, each next to another—
now here we are taking them down.

We take all the frames, leave some pictures.
Because we can't put a name to the face.
All the while, we're smiling, the music's up loud,
and the heat she loved up we've turned down.

Why do I save all these ticket stubs?
Postcards? The leaves from a hike?
Just so someone could come when my time here is done—
and throw it all into the trash.

The Dust Settles

I am a ship once sturdy
but taking on water now
fast
every drop
another's pain
it all flows in
waves (and waves)
until my hull snaps in two
righteous anger
I am submerged
in water (in pain)
it seeps into my bones
rusts my anchor.

I am nestled at the bottom of the sea
where the pressure would destroy me
but I was already rotting, already two, already crushed
by the first drop of water I touched.

The ground isn't hard, but it hurts my knees
as six dogwoods blow flowers into the breeze.
Black rivers.
All I see are black rivers.
Earth and ashes and dust and
black rivers flowing over stone.

The Dust Settles

She sleeps

with the window open

so she's closer to the stars

and closer to the ones she's lost.

You're drowning,

but you don't scream.

What good would it do?

There's no boat

no people

not a ray of hope or rescue.

There's no one left to throw a raft

or hold your hand

or say a prayer—

so you tread

like you've always done

like you'll always do.

You have to learn to swim when you're alone.

I keep imagining a world you haven't left. The phone calls, the texts, the dinner table conversations that stretch long after dinner. I keep imagining a world still filled with PMS chocolate bars and crushed donut boxes in the outside garbage cans. Every milestone—and every average, normal day—I picture you there: sitting, watching, laughing until you cough. You would love our new puppy and hate my new car. What would you say, if you saw me graduate college? And then do it again? Would you be proud? Or apprehensive thinking of the five long years of doctoral work we face? If you saw me surrounded by books along the way, tears in my eyes and deadlines long gone by, would you tell me it'll be alright, or sit down beside me and work through it all with me? If you saw me up on that amphitheater stage in the bright colored lights singing for a crowd of 10,000, would you be proud? Or grinding your teeth, hanging on every note, more nervous than me? But then, you'd've been up there with me, and I wouldn't have been nervous at all. If you saw me standing in your recording studio, surrounded by your equipment, looking lost— If you saw me stranded in the middle of a restaurant with no idea why your speakers cut out on me— If you saw me crouched in the corner of my bedroom, tears streaming thick and fast down my face, clutching a broken string to the fragile neck of the guitar we built together, rocking and whispering to myself: *it's okay, you're okay, it's okay, you're okay*— Would you lie and say it would all be okay? Would you even know you were lying? But then, you'd've just whisked it away and brought it back all in one piece. And I never would have cried over a broken string if you were alive.

I can't shorten the strap on your guitar.
I didn't think it would be this hard.
I can't put away the last guitar you played
but I know you'd want it in its case.
So I'm sorry.
I'm sure you're cringing now.
Thinking I've thrown away any hope
(and maybe I have?)
because your mic stand is still a foot too tall
and that twelve-string is still up on the wall
I can't change a thing, I can't—
I can't.
I can't. I can't.
Not without the leader of the band.

For all the hours in the day, I listen to other people's lives. Their problems and their fears, their thoughts, opinions, feelings— I don't care for the answers, but I ask the questions. How are you thinking about—? What are you feeling about—? What is your perspective on—? But what is my perspective? Do I get a perspective? Because I'm not sure I do.

So I write the things. The thoughts that others think aloud and ask me to think on paper right back at them. And I do the things. The things that others tell me to do, expect me to do, want me to do. And I say the words. The words that others said to me, the words that made me feel like a person for the only time in my life. But I don't mean them. And I wonder if he even meant them. Because I am saying them for their benefit, not for mine. Not because they're true.

So am I a person? If I have no personhood? Am I even thinking if my thoughts are not my own? Am I a good writer, a good speaker, a good friend if I don't mean the words I choose? Or just a good actor? A good rememberer of when I was a person too?

I don't understand rivers
how they keep flowing
forever and ever.
They are past, present, future
relics of villages past—
prayers for the future—
fertility and healing and growth—
But all we'll ever see is the present.
How do they go on?
All this time?
How do they see the generations come and go
and still flow with hope?

This month, my sister will walk down the aisle of our family church alone. She has been fantasizing about this day since she was a little girl: the white dress, the flowers, the whole family packed into the pews, my father at her side. But now that the day is fast-approaching, we know: She will walk down the aisle alone.

When my sister and I drove together, erratically, into the city, when we made it there too late, when we held our father's callused hands as the warmth left them forever, when we felt our spines sag and our souls disintegrate, my sister's hand was bare.

We stopped that night for milk. We had run out, and my mother needed it for her coffee the next morning. She half-walked, half-jogged into the flickering fluorescent lights of the 7/11 while my sister and I sat, now too close together without my mother at my other side, emailing our professors in the back of my uncle's Prius. I was struck by the normalcy of it all. How obstinate is the mundane! Even when someone dies, coffee needs milk, professors need explanations.

We mourned, and cried, and honored his short life, and the next Monday, we went back to school. We wrote essays and took midterms and, in some classes, when it was absolutely necessary, we participated.

Somewhere along the line, stopping for milk at 7/11 turned into returning to class. Returning to class turned into celebrating Christmas, going on family vacations, and seeing my soon-to-be brother-in-law slip a ring on my sister's left hand. Because joy and life itself are, in the end, just as obstinate as the mundane. And, somewhere along the line, the 7/11 parking lot became the aisle.

The parking lot alone became the aisle alone, and we continue on.

The soles of my feet have been rubbed raw
scrubbed by sandpaper shoes
burning and twinging with every step.
But moving is all I know how to do
the only way to stop thinking for a moment
to forget the hurricane inside my head
and see the blue sky outside myself.
I must walk

run

move

so I guess I'll just buy a new pair of shoes.

I picture myself with gray in my hair,

lines on my face around my eyes and my mouth

but my eyes—

but my smile—

they both seem to shout

I am so happy! (now)

I look happier.

I hope I'm happier

then.

I hope, by then, I don't feel empty inside

I hope, by then, I think of life

as something not so serious at all

I hope, by then, I've settled into

my own skin

and my own hands,

and I hope the pulsing emptiness inside my chest is filled

by then.

What constitutes emptiness?
The caverns are empty, I suppose,
but aren't they full?
Full of stalactites and stalagmites,
full of stone.
Underground rivers wind through cavern floors
and underground waterfalls crash from one hundred feet (or more)
So how could the cavern be empty,
with a whole world nestled inside?

What constitutes silence?
For echoes rest in every curve of the cavern walls
settled into the cracks and dents in the surface of the stone
and one tap of a hanging cone
reverberates until the cavern itself screams.
So how could the cavern be silent
when it's absorbed centuries of sound?
When it is sound itself?

Am I empty? Am I silent?
Or have I stopped letting people in
to see the rivers and falls in my chest
to hear the echoes in my head—
Have I stopped letting myself in?

2

the wind slows
but doesn't cease
and just when you think
you can finally breathe
another gust hits
face lashed by wet hair whips
dust and sand lodged
under heavy eyelids
can't speak
can't think
can't breathe
praying for another lull
this is the middle

In the face of death
we are born again
infants again
helpless and hopeless
confused and lost
and dependent:
unable to get out of bed
dependent on others
to tug us gently from our sheets
unable to feed ourselves
dependent on others
to bring lasagnas and mac and cheese
unable to self-soothe
dependent on others
to handle even emotions.
One person's circle of life,
it seems,
rewinds all the circles nearest to it
until we are all toothless teetering
infants again
helpless and hopeless
confused and lost

My dad drank two cups of coffee while he read the newspaper each morning. Just milk, no sugar. (Except for that one time he poured milk on his waffles and syrup in his coffee.) And so, on the morning of October 10, 2017, my sister and I had one cup of coffee each. So my mom wouldn't have to pour his coffee down the drain. And we each had one cup of coffee every morning since. And now I get headaches if I skip my cup, so even if I'm not home, even if I'm not with my mom at all, I still have my coffee. It has become routine. And I wonder, now, how much of my everyday life, how many little things, changed forever without my knowing it (on the morning of October 10, 2017).

We've grown used to cooking half a box of pasta. My sister grills. My mother blows out the sprinklers. I fill up my own windshield washer fluid now. When a storm rages outside and a flash of lightning fills the still house, when the lights flicker off and on, we reset the clocks ourselves. And we don't even notice.

I no longer notice when I sit in the back seat alone, my mom having moved to the driver's seat and my sister to the passenger's—a counterclockwise bereavement recalibration. I no longer notice that the orange juice bottle in the refrigerator is always full; no longer notice that the rows and rows of DVDs are all covered in dust.

We bought a new couch, a new kitchen table, a new cushioned chair. There are no empty spots left screaming *he should be here!*

Superbowl Sunday morning,
I couldn't find your Giants jersey.
I sought, specifically, your Simms jersey,
but when I found none—
I guess I have no right to cry,
to sink down into a heap on the floor
with the belts and the shoes and the neckties,
if it took me four and a half years to look.

Grieving is losing your favorite shirt.

It's almost a relief to know it's really gone.

You know you won't waste time anymore

searching.

You know, now, there's no more doubt.

You won't wake up anymore, and plan

to wear the shirt

because it's gone.

No more disappointment

No more surprises

No more grief—

You only have to lose it once.

But then, aren't you losing it every day?

Every day that it's not there,

don't you miss it?

Don't you always think

I know what shirt would be perfect— If only.

You only have to grieve once, sure,

but the grieving never ends.

The Dust Settles

There is no badge
that we are given
that says *Please note: I am sad.*
There is no mask
that we are given
to help us hide the sad.
But wouldn't it be nice?
To announce, or to completely hide,
instead of existing in this liminal space
of dark circles and greasy hair
of bitten nails and blotchy faces
of falling apart and failing to care.
It feels indecent, impolite, improper
to show such misery to the world—
to let this creature out in public,
and let the innocent watch as its
grotesque tentacles unfurl.

It's in the fourth year, I've learned, that people stop caring
stop thinking
stop remembering.
They've settled into the loss,
and they expect I have, too.
His name, his person, has been filed as deceased in their minds,
and they can hardly remember a time it wasn't.
So—
First the gifts stop—
the fruit baskets and the cardinal décor.
Then the phone calls stop, exchanged for texts.
But the texts shrivel, shorter and shorter—
a handful of *thinking of yous*
replace the heartfelt paragraphs that used to flow like water.
And then, in the fourth year,
even the *thinking of yous* stop.

I don't remember my eighteenth birthday, but I remember my nineteenth, my sister's twenty-fifth. I remember the giftbag sitting on the pillow of my cousins' guest room on the 47th floor, the pink tissue paper startling in my dim world. I remember the weight of the books I pulled out of that giftbag, and I remember the feel of them smashing against my lower back for the rest of the weekend as I speed walked down Manhattan streets. I remember the smell of ammonia, and I remember my dad, fighting through the morphine every time his nurse came in his room just to tell her it was his daughters' birthday. I remember him apologizing, though I still don't know what for. I remember my birthday dinner, a diner in Harlem, one block away from the hospital. A hurried dinner— I remember picking at my penne ala vodka and wondering why my mom didn't stop me from ordering penne ala vodka from a diner. I remember watching her pull veins from her chicken. I remember the crippling guilt when we made it back to the hospital only to find out that my dad had been awake and asking for us while we were gone, though I'm not sure the word *remember* is accurate when I am still crippled by that guilt. And I remember that night, walking back to the apartment with my cousins, trying to convince them (read: myself) that this next round of chemo was going to cure him once and for all. And I remember them kindly feigning excitement at the good news, and I remember stopping at Duane Reade, and I remember my cousin buying me a whole bag of Reese's shaped like pumpkins. I remember trying to get him to accept my limp ten-dollar bill. I remember trying to act like an adult when my whole body was aching to be held by my dad. And I remember, thirty-six hours later, walking into a room with four bodies and three souls, and feeling my own soul crumble into pieces.

"a beautiful little fool"
but I don't think foolishness
is the answer.
The answer is callousness.
Cold-heartedness.
Selfishness.
The answer is to lack the
capacity for reflection.
The answer is ignorant confidence,
universal disregard.
Because if foolishness is the answer
then knowledge is the problem—
but it is not knowledge,
intelligence, understanding,
that rips my heart from my chest;
it is caring.
I hope my daughter
is a beautiful little callous,
cold-hearted, selfish girl—
and I wish I was, too.

Sometimes

I want to curl up into a ball

like an armadillo

and wait for the storm inside me to pass

but I don't think it works like that.

The only way out is through.

But what on earth does that mean?

I slept through a luau when I was six years old, and when I woke my father put leis on his neck and on his ankles and his wrists and did his best to reenact the luau I missed. I miss the big things: Christmas mornings and Father's Days. But I miss the little things more. An elevator luau and a Planet of the Apes marathon. Playing castaways on couch cushions on the living room floor and pouring two glasses of milk with brownies instead of just one. I miss the normalcy of having my dad in my life.

Why am I writing these poems?
Why am I kicking up the little bit of dust
that has already settled?
I used to be able to see photos
and not cry—
and now here am I:
cowering
sobbing
rocking
strangled in the corner just
because I saw a photograph—
with those deep lines of laughter
and my ache for the past
has consumed me again.

I pull the excess thread

through to the inside of my sweater

unseen but still present

not healed

not restored

not the way it had been—

before

You're sad (because he's gone).
You're mad (because he said he'd be fine.
And he swore he'd never lie.
Everything I say is, by definition, a promise).

You're confused;
Twenty-two long months of chemo and radiation and
hospitals and transplants and gloves and masks and
get well cards and fear hidden behind nervous jokes
twenty-two months—
But now,
—now?—
his body can't handle it anymore?

Yes, you're mad. (And you're ashamed that you're mad.)

And you're lost, as you sit in the passenger seat and look
back at the city that stole him;
as you pile books on his chair to hide the empty;
as you brush the dust off the guitar and
wear the strap too long.
It's a new world, and a scary place.

Sad. Mad. Confused. Mad. Lost.
And somewhere: relieved.
Because now you can be sad and mad and
ashamed and confused and mad and lost
without being worried, too.

And you'll go on
being sad and mad and confused and mad and lost
but not worried
until one day you forget that you're
sad and mad and ashamed and confused and mad and lost

But then you'll open those double doors
and they'll squeak just like every morning (before.)
and pinewood and spearmint will hit you like a wall
and bring you to your knees
and you'll be sad and mad and ashamed and
confused and mad and lost
and worried
all over again.

I fear I've climbed a mountain
and I made it to the top.
I fear I've climbed a mountain
though I started with no gear.
With every mile on my way
I found a harness and a rope
a helmet and a safety vest
a compass and a map.
I fear I've climbed a mountain
and when I made it to the top
I passed my gear back down the trail
to those just starting out.
I fear I've climbed a mountain
and given away my gear
only to find that the mountain I've climbed
is only beginning here.

The meter in my chest counts the seconds since you left
and I've lost count, but surely it did not.
The meter in my chest counts the seconds since you left
since it has been fragmented
broken in pieces, strewn between ribs
and if I run fast enough I hear the pieces clanging
like broken glass.
But the meter in my chest that counts the seconds since you left
still ticks.

The Dust Settles

I remember his white polka dotted short sleeve button down shirt.
I was six days shy of sixteen,
heartbroken and sure I would never survive
the gut-wrenching loss of a friend.
And he came and he picked me up from school,
and he was still in his work clothes,
his white polka dotted short sleeve button down shirt
over his uniform to hide his badge
and we ate cheeseburgers and French fries, and we cried.
I found that shirt today,
his white polka dotted short sleeve button down shirt.
But the polka dots are squares.

How much else have I forgotten?

I am disappointed in humanity.
I've had that moment, where Dorothy
sees behind the curtain, and knows
the wizard is not what she'd hoped.
Humanity is not what I'd hoped,
not what I thought,
not what it was, once,
when my father was a part of it.
The magic's gone with him,
and the good of the world, too,
and we are stuck with a humanity full
of people too corrupt
for heaven to ever want.

Leviathan Lucifer Beelzebub
I can feel two small spikes in my hair
my tongue's forking babbling spinning spitting
and my eyes have now reddened and squared.

Kindness is cornered in the echoing chamber
of my rapidly blackening chest
I throw love on the fire to quench anger with water—
but find love is gasoline instead.

I love you I love you I love you, I'm sorry
The flesh peels away from my face.
My thin lips curl up— *do all things in love*
Let the monster, now, out of his cage.

The guilt comes before
the rage fully leaves,
and in guilt's presence, the rage
turns in on me.
In your arms, in your arms, in your arms,
I am cooled. I am calmed.
The rhythm of your heart
and the steady strength of your arms
are holy water. salt. sage.

I have decided to (attempt to) prioritize the people that I love. Which, I know, sounds straightforward and simple, but apparently it's not. Because I spent the last twenty-three years caring about everyone, worrying about everyone, spending energy on everyone. And for the last twenty-three years this has eaten away at me and my soul, left me crumpled and shaking until I was nothing but anger and hatred, lashing out at the people that I love. Because, I've learned, some people are like colanders, and no matter how much love you pour into them, you can never love them into something of substance. You cannot slit your own wrists to pour every drop of bleeding love into a colander. And so, by ceasing to pour love into everyone regardless of their steely holes, by refusing to give time, love, and energy to everyone I come into contact with, I can save the best parts of myself for the people that I love. I will take the love I pour into people like colanders, incapable of retaining any form of love, selfish to the core, and I will give all of that love to the people who deserve it. And it seems selfish, and callous, and coldhearted, but I don't think it is; I think it is just a form of conservation. I will conserve love for people who will retain it rather than pour it down the drain. I will be a conservationist of love.

The air smells thick and warm

sharp sounds—the clang of stacked pots

the chime of dog tags—

rounded in the thick air.

Overpowered by the turning of the newspaper pages

the first splash of coffee into a rounded mug.

This is where you cry.

This is where you drop your bags,

kick off your shoes.

This is where you let down your guard,

and let laughter rip up through your stomach

and bounce off the walls,

and this is where you cry.

The sun is bright and hot on my skin. My chest is filled with something— heavy with lightness. The air is fresh in my bruised lungs. My eyes are not drooping— aching— stinging—
What a change!
I wonder: is this happiness? or the absence of sadness?
why so infrequent? why so evasive? is it me? is it my choices? is it the people I think I love? think I need?
who makes the sun feel dull and cold? why does my chest fill with emptiness— weaken with heaviness? how is the air stagnant in my bruised lungs? why are my eyes drooping, aching, stinging—
every other moment but now?

a wiffle ball bat
in someone else's grass
and I am transported back:
a patio chair for a strike zone
the tire swing first base
invisible man on third—
and it's outta here!—
and Pepper steals the ball and runs
and my mom is calling us for dinner now
but tomorrow we'll be back

Does it all equal out in the end? Does the good ever outweigh the bad? I have never felt joy as strongly as I feel pain. Even before all the deaths. Even at a young age. Joy has never been as plentiful as pain. So maybe, if it all evens out, it's just unevenly dispersed. Maybe my first bite of life was heavy on the bad, but the good is coming later. Or maybe it doesn't even out. Maybe my life just has more pain than joy. Or maybe this in itself is the problem. Maybe I'm not supposed to keep score.

But can the good ever outweigh the bad? Because the formula is rigged. No matter how good the good is, the badness of the bad is greater than or equal to the goodness of the good, because we will inevitably lose the good, which will ultimately invert the goodness into an equal amount of badness. Therefore:

[the badness of life] = –[the good] + [the other bad things]

which means that we maybe might one day even out at zero (if [the other bad things] = 0), but the good can never outweigh the bad.

But correct me if I'm wrong; math was never my strongest subject.

With my head on your chest
I can hear your steady heart
and I am jealous.
To feel steady and sure,
to not feel my chest
caving in on itself around a
shrunken, quivering heart.
Your arms are wrapped tight around me—
one hand in my hair,
the other on my back,
and I feel peace,
but interwoven through peace is guilt that
I am so jealous of your heart at ease.

When the guitars exchanged their honey tones for buzzing, he popped the batteries out and, for good measure, gently touched the edge of the 9-volt battery to the tip of his tongue. Every time, dead or alive, he made the same face: scrunched, wincing eyes and a crinkled nose for a fraction of a second. And we always laughed. And when (in the middle of a party, with two hundred eyes fixed on me, with no father to be found on earth, with tears threatening to spill over my mascara lashes and betray the burning sorrow inside me) buzzing replaced my guitar's honey tones, it was my sister who touched the tip of her tongue to the 9-volt battery. Her wince was violent, and she coughed as she whispered, *it tasted like a jalapeño.*

It is times like these, lost and confused and overwhelmed, tears and sweat mixing together on the thin-skinned purple circles under my eyes, that I think the burning sadness inside me might ignite my whole body until I explode and my grief shoots debris into the air. But I didn't lose the only person who cared (like I thought I did). I have my sister. And no matter how distraught I am, how close to exploding I am, *it tasted like a jalapeño* will always be funny.

no one will throw a life raft

no one will throw a rope

not because they don't care

but because they don't know

for I keep swearing I'm not drowning

keep swearing I can swim

I look back on the past
a childhood full of laughter
joy and safety;
I look forward
eager to have my own children
to provide them with lives
full of laughter joy and safety;
and I forget that I have a now
a here and a now
a life right now
laughter joy and safety
now.

I am not sure who I am—

thoughts trapped and spiraling—

hurtling through negatives—

scratching at my skin—

picking at my scalp—

chewing at my lips—

but sometimes

motionless.

catatonic.

The paralysis comes as a relief.

a numb after the motion.

unwinding.

unraveling.

unhappy.

un.

unhuman.

But when you are here, the energy returns—

unhindered joy replaces anxiety—

dancing running laughing singing—

constant motion constant joy—

and I don't care anymore—

who I am or who I think I am—

because I am alive—

and my sister is here.

The air carries the click of the stove
the warm sounds of water running into a pot
perfumed by the floury smell of
bubbling, boiling penne.
She runs laps around the kitchen:
Refrigerator, counter, stove,
refrigerator, counter, stove,
refrigerator again.
We don't talk, for I am nestled in
a pile of blankets and pillows
one room away,
but the rounded sounds,
the warm, cozy air,
the smells of love—
From one room away, I know
I am safe.

I am a woman of faith. I believe in God and in Jesus Christ, and I believe that the dead will rise. I believe in heaven, and I believe in earth, and I believe in stopping, taking note of how much the people in your life are worth. I have an incredible mother, a provider and a nurturer, selfless and humble and strong. I have never met anyone as selfless and humble and strong as she is. I am lucky to have her, lucky to be her daughter. My sister is my best friend, simultaneously witty and dopey, and my partner in everything that we do. I am lucky to have her. I am lucky to have them both. I believe in relationships. I believe that's all we really have, or at least all we have that really matters. What good is a job, a house, a car, without the people you love? And I believe I will see my father again. I don't know if there really are gates made of pearl, if the streets really are made of gold. But I imagine heaven is just a dish of my mom's cooking at the table in my childhood home, sitting across from my sister, my mother at my left, my father at my right. I hope heaven is just having everyone I love back together, under one roof, around one kitchen table, breaking bread. All together again.

Rivers are really just love

flowing with love

overflowing with love

love for the lost generations

but love, too, for the new

because love, now, is flowing

through my veins

welling up in my eyes

love for my father, yes,

but love, too, for my mother

my sister

my aunts my uncles

my cousins my friends

I am so lucky

my river still flows

with hope?

no, with love.

My sister did not walk down the aisle alone.

My mother held her arm, and

they walked together

and— we weren't alone in the parking lot

of that 7/11 that night

my mother may have run inside, but

we had each other

sister. aunt. uncle.

taken in as one of their own

we were together

maybe we always were

I don't think we're alone

maybe we never were

3

not every gust

stirs up the dust

but some do

and some always will

but in the moments

when the wind is not blowing

rub your eyes

pull back your hair

speak

think

breathe

even in this desert

there is peace

this is the healing

I am still struck by the image of desert rocks,
worn away into disproportionate, jagged, tottering shapes,
climbing disjointedly toward an open sky.
Weathered by the dust in the wind.
I am those rocks; those rocks are me.
Shaped and formed by the desert storms,
and forever changed.
The dust will settle, the winds will cease,
but my jagged new edges will remain.
For better or for worse, I myself am changed.
Still, *the dust settles*.

"Pans!" Every Saturday morning at 7am. Like clockwork. Sometimes a text message, sometimes a shout up the staircase— but, usually, both. "Who shall have this first fine batch of pancakes," spatula in hand, thick, yellow batter dripping down the kitchen cabinets, "and who shall have the son of the batch?"

His spot at the table is empty now, and the cabinets haven't been coated in batter in years, but his love still fills the kitchen every Saturday morning as we laugh and recite all his usually Saturday quotes— over a *fine batch of pancakes*, of course.

Shedding fibers

soft strands of polyester

pulled through thin mesh

this fragile thing I've won

I've won

me

and as thumb caresses

delicate comfort

I smell popcorn butter the air

hear festival bells

feel the weight of moisture in a night

two hundred miles and a decade away:

a green terrycloth dragon with purple horns

Cava, he called her,

made us promise to share her

she was sturdier, that terrycloth dragon

he won for us

but this fragile thing I've won.

I am smart

I am capable

I can take care of myself

I am smart

I am capable

I can take care of myself

I can have weak moments and not be weak

I can have dumb moments and not be dumb

I can have lazy moments and not be lazy

I can have mean moments and not be mean

I can have crazy moments and not be crazy

We are not defined by our every moment

I am not defined by my every moment

Life is not scripted—

We have room for error

We are not defined by our every moment.

I am not defined by my every moment.

and in the stillness of the rolling hills

in the rabbits in the tall grass

in the breeze that lets the branches relax

and release (tiny white petals to drift through the trees)

I think I can finally

begin

to

breathe

Instead of putting his eyeglasses on his head or tucking them into his shirt, he stuck them on his forehead— I don't think we have a picture of that. He kept his nails cut short, below his fingertips, and his hands were covered in calluses— I don't think we have a picture of that. He answered the phone with "*Yellow*," he sneezed so loud the neighbors heard, he coughed when he laughed really hard, he hummed a note until he matched it on his guitar— I don't think we have a video of that. And so, if I am the only record of the antics and the mannerisms and the person who was once so alive, then let it be known: He put a finger to the red mole on his temple and said he was getting a message from his home planet; he did headstands in the kitchen but toppled over onto his side just when you started to get impressed; he couldn't bear to see a crooked picture or a flashing digital clock, and he adjusted both photos and clocks everywhere he went; he didn't build our backyard shed, but he'd like you to think he did; he smiled a pained smile, wide-lipped and dead-eyed, when someone sang out of key; he loved bright and sunny summer days because the movie theaters were empty; he loved to play his guitar while he watched the Mets; he loved, for a time, mustard pretzels and iced coffee; he loved his dog; he loved his wife; he loved his daughters.

She said to choose the characteristic

that I miss most

and adopt it as my own,

be for others the person I miss.

But how can I be kind and funny

and smart and loving and witty and goofy

and wise and understanding and accepting

and speak softly and laugh loudly

all at the same time?

Why couldn't he just be kind?

That would be easier.

Just funny? Just smart?

Just loving, witty, goofy, wise, understanding, accepting?

Just one good thing?

Why did he leave such big shoes to fill?

And why did someone so genuinely good

die?

I might
(maybe) be
(a little bit) sad
forever.
And that might
(maybe)
be okay.

at the moment I dipped under

saltwater in my mouth

decided to give up

at the moment I began to drown

she threw a raft

threw a rope

and pulled me back on board

and she doesn't even know

Darts, to me, the way I play, is a game of luck. I don't know how to stand, or how to hold the dart, or where to look. And somehow, in this game of luck, I hit the double bullseye (once), that little tiny red dot in the center of the green comparatively-larger-but-still-tiny bullseye in the center. My next dart didn't even make it to the board, and I believe it is still lodged in the basement floor. But still. I hit the double bullseye (once).

That's what I need to focus on, I think. What I need to realize. Speaking metaphorically, of course, because some people actually know how to throw a dart: Not every dart will make it to the board. Some will wedge themselves in the wall and get me in trouble, some in the floor and get me in trouble *and* made fun of. Some will make it to the board, but nowhere near center. But that doesn't mean I'll never hit double-bull. I lost my dad. That's a dart in the wall. I dropped a burrito between my driver's seat and my center console. That's a dart in the floor. I am exhausted, bored of life. That's a dart on the board, nowhere near bullseye. But I have an amazing mom, a best friend and a sister in one, an aunt and uncle who have taken me in as one of their own children, and I had wonderful, wonderful grandparents and a wonderful, wonderful father. They are my double-bull darts. Maybe my dad-as-double-bullseye-dart was pulled out of its place, but it still happened. Not all of my darts are lodged in the hardwood floor.

You're allowed to say mean things

and hate the world

and cry with anger at the world

and feel so full of despair

that you don't know if you'll make it out alive

And you're allowed to cry so hard the tears cover your whole face

drip down your neck

down your chest

And you're allowed to feel like the world is caving in and burning

all at the same time

And you're allowed to wonder if you'll even make it

through the night

And you're allowed to succumb to the darkness without looking

at the bright side

without making the most of it

without trying to see things through a different lens

You're allowed to feel, even when feeling hurts

You're allowed to feel, even if it makes others uncomfortable

I don't leave footprints,
but I know the ground I walk on
is changed by my steps.
No pebble, no grain of sand
is where it was before me, before my footfall.
And in my simple way, that no one will notice,
I leave my mark.
I am heading somewhere great—
or maybe nowhere at all,
but the shoes that rub my heels remind me I am walking
and I forget that I am *going*.
Remind me I am working
and I forget that I am *living*.
Remind me I am hurting
and I forget that I am *feeling*.

soft Martin scales

the smell of rosewood and mahogany

I am there— everywhere

the backyard, the couch

the studio, the golf club

and propane—

Grandma's house—

scratch cake and sticky placemats

chocolate milk and bubble gum

reading *Ferdinand the Bull*

Oh, if I could live in the warm embrace

if I could be swallowed up by the sweet smells

of memories

I am grateful for my parents, not because they put us first, but because they put us even with one another from the start. Their date nights were Monopoly, sitting crisscross on the floor. And we were all my father's Valentines, year after year after year. We were homemade birthday cakes, we were long family walks, we were television all together at night, four in a row on the couch. We were "What do you want to do with—?" We were "What do you think about—?" We were *everybody gets a say*. We were one family unit, not two parents vs. two kids. No selfish/selfless, us vs. them. Four was a prime number back then. We could not be broken down. Just a happy family of four, playing Monopoly on the living room floor.

There are friends I will love

that I haven't met yet.

There are places I will see in person

that I haven't seen in photographs yet.

There are books I will write

that I haven't thought of yet.

There are fun facts I will love

that haven't been discovered yet.

There are mentors that will change my life

that haven't been hired yet.

There are articles that I will print and save, read again and again

that haven't been researched yet.

There are books that will make me feel all kinds of feelings

whose authors haven't learned the alphabet yet.

There are stories that will make me laugh so hard I cry

that haven't happened yet.

There are people that I will love more than life itself

that haven't been born yet.

There is a future, a life I will love,

that is still

totally and utterly

yet to come.

the same bird calls have woken me
every morning for the past twenty-three years
cardinal, mourning dove, black-capped chickadee
and I never stopped to think,
stopped to realize, that maybe
I've been gently woken by twenty generations
the songs were the same, but the singers themselves
had to have changed, and this comforts me
though I'm not sure if I am comforted by the notion
that stability is just an illusion
or that the next generation might stand a chance
at replenishing what we've lost

The sun is setting over the bluffs. I can see the ferry lights in the distance and the wavering ripples of the Sound shimmering with the dock lights. The saltwater droplets in the breeze are refreshing after summer's first heat. And I feel peace. There is an absence, a gaping black hole in my chest that sucks my stomach up into it until I am empty inside— most of the time. But now, the emptiness feels like lightness (or maybe it really is lightness), and I think maybe one day I might feel whole again. Even if *one day* is far away. Even if *one day* is, maybe, today.

we're waiting on the world to end:

sitting here watching

pink and orange, dying breaths

tomorrow it will begin again

another shore, another life

we'll know east from west

sound from ocean

today from tomorrow

joy from mourning

When things were fresh—my wounds, my grief, the overturned dirt on my father's grave—happiness was nonexistent. Not faint, but absent entirely. The first time I laughed, a wave of guilt coursed through my chest, up to my throat, and swallowed the laugh whole. How could I betray my father by laughing in a world without him? But as years went on, I laughed more. And more. And more. I still feel gutted every June, reminded I am fatherless each Father's Day—but no, *reminded* is not the right word, because I always remember; I never forget my dad, and I never forget this gaping loss. But sometimes—in fact, now, often—I am able to focus on the good far more than I focus on the bad. When I think of my dad, I now picture him with hair. Full-faced and joyful. Strong. Healthy. Maybe healing isn't forgetting the bad altogether. Maybe this is healing. And maybe there is no such thing as *healed*, only *healing*.

lying in the hot sun with a cool breeze,
in the short silence before each wave breaks,
I find peace.

I think I know now

what she meant

those rainy afternoons

when she had said

the only way out is through.

I thought then

of course

there is no path but through

but no

hundreds of paths unfold:

avoidance

withdrawal

escapism

stifled sorrow

masked sorrow

misguided sorrow

unexplored sorrow

and to journey through

you must *be*

be sad

be angry

be present

I tried so desperately to heal

I never allowed myself to feel

I saw a mourning dove today
on the corner of the street, below a shady tree.
I recognized her pale pink breast
and the curves around her eyes.
I thought she would leave me
that she would startle and fly away,
but she just stared as I approached,
and stared as I walked by.
It was a brief encounter.
I didn't hesitate, didn't miss a stride,
but I feel I saw an old friend (in the curves around her eyes).
I used to love the dove's low coo,
but today she was silent (I was silent too),
and she and I, I think, both saw each other for who we are,
once mourners, always mourners, but, today, at peace—
on the corner of the street, below a shady tree.

We must be at the beach. The north shore, not the south, facing west, to see the sun dip into the water of the Sound. But all around us, across the whole sky, for long after the sun sinks into the horizon, the sky is streaked with pink. And the beauty of your life is not confined to those who knew you, because everyone who knows we who loved you is indirectly touched by the light of your life:

I go to great lengths for a joke; Sam knows every player on the '86 Mets (who played six years before her birth); my mom spares no expense for family and slows down, now, to enjoy the day to day; Uncle Anthony looks with his ears, not his eyes, when he picks the strings of his guitar; Aunt Eydie will drop everything, do anything, for everyone she knows; Uncle Jerry— I wonder how much of him is from you, and how much of you was from him, for your brains are one in the same, and I have a second father in him; Uncle Charles can transpose a song on the fly, and half the quotes that come out of his mouth have come from yours, too, at some time; Aunt Denise tells a story with props; Aunt Maddy is a listener, and listens with her heart wide open, focuses every ounce of her attention on whomever it is that needs her; Uncle Chris has the ear, hums a harmony note, and keeps a straight face to expand on a joke in exactly the same way as you; and Charlie tries to dream up the most efficient innovations (a remnant from his time at Red Maple Road), and his ease of conversation relaxes those around him; and Diana has your mannerisms: her facial expressions before splitting into a grin; and Billy holds his laughs inside his face, and can fix anything that we break; and Joey can logic his way through anything, and holds his logic in his hands for all to see; and Michael believes in doing what he loves, and uses stories to remember the words in a song; and Melissa's voice—her language, the shape of her vowels, and her sense of humor itself—are all echoes of you; and Jackie is steady and calm and kind, there for everyone, kind to everyone, and everything she touches is art: her heart and her brain are yours.

We are your pink streaks, stretching far and wide across the sky.

Resources

My hope with this collection was to extend a literary hand to my fellow grievers of the world and, hopefully, help you in some small way—help you to see that you're not alone, or help you to see that there is no right or wrong way to grieve. I do not, however, pretend to believe that one tiny little book is enough to console a broken heart.

While writing and playing music helped me through my grief the most, my mother found the most support through community—her local bereavement counseling group and online Facebook groups. There is something that will help you, but remember that not everything will help everyone. If you find the first thing that you try does not help you, please, please keep looking for that something that will.

The following pages contain some resources to help grievers like you and me as we navigate our new lives.

Books

Grief is a Journey Kenneth J. Doka

Grief is Love: Living with Loss Marisa Renee Lee

The Modern Loss Handbook: An Interactive Guide to Moving Through Grief and Building your Resilience Rebecca Soffer

Option B Sheryl Sandberg and Adam Grant

When You're Ready, This Is How You Heal Brianna Wiest

Wouldn't Take Nothing from My Journey Now Maya Angelou

Podcasts

New Day Claire Bidwell Smith

In Your Feelings thoughtcatalogue

Good Mourning Sal and Im

Grief Is My Superpower Mark Lemon

Websites

The Artist's Grief Deck griefdeck.com

Grief Narratives griefnarratives.com

HealGrief healgrief.org

Modern Loss modernloss.com

Option B optionb.org

Remembering a Life rememberingalife.com

What's Your Grief? whatsyourgrief.com

Seeking Bereavement Counseling

Many places near you likely offer bereavement counseling. Reach out to the following places near you to see if bereavement counseling is being offered. (Often, these services are offered to everyone in the community regardless of whether you used their services or not.)

- Local hospice centers
- Local funeral homes
- Local churches

You can also use the online **Dougy Center Bereavement Support Directory** to enter your zip code and find bereavement counseling being offered near you.

There are also many bereavement groups and pages available on social media sites such as Facebook for you to find community amongst us fellow grievers.

Activities to Promote Peace and Healing

Exercising

Walking, especially outside among nature

Yoga

Journaling

Writing a letter to your lost loved one

Playing an instrument or listening to music

Gardening

Creating visual art (painting, sculpting, drawing, coloring, etc.)

Cooking or baking (cooking your loved one's favorite meal may help you to feel a connection to them)

Author's Note

As I organized this collection, I was extremely hesitant to create the sections as they appear in this publication. Section one, "the beginning," is marked by feelings of disorientation, fog, confusion, and feeling alone and overwhelmed. When I reflect on this period of my grieving process, this period of my life, I cannot remember much of what I was thinking, feeling, or doing. It's a blur. Section two, "the middle," is my journey back to humanity, learning to trust those around me while sorting through anger toward them and fear of losing them, too. Section three, "the healing," is when my grief ceases to be the focal point of my life and the key component of my identity. These are all accurate representations of my journey through these first five years following my father's death.

The issue with this formatting, however, is that it does not accurately depict the blurred lines between these periods. In my experience, I had to move through the disoriented, foggy period in order to interact with other people again, and I had to interact with other people again in order to reach the "healing" period. However, these "periods" do not end altogether; even the "healing" phase often circles back to points from the beginning and the middle. The disorientation phase and my anger toward those around me did not completely vanish with time, but, rather, the trips back to disorientation and anger grew briefer and less incapacitating. In my experience, grief and the impacts of grief on everyday life never really cease (perhaps because the intense love that led to such intense grief doesn't fade after death). Instead of trying to get over our grief, then, we need to accept our grief and (try to) find peace in it. We also, however, need to accept ourselves and be kind to ourselves; we need to understand that it is okay to still be sad, and it is completely normal for us to experience anger, and experiencing some of "the beginning," and "the middle" feelings does not mean that you're regressing.

Human beings have such a deep capacity for love. We are social beings, who experience deep attachments to the people in our lives. Losing one of these people is not just difficult, it is life-changing. The purpose of this book is to show the many conflicting emotions that I experienced during my grieving process. It is not to suggest that there are "stages" to grief (an old theory that has since been modified). I want this collection to provide hope and comfort to readers; I want you to know that you are not alone; I want you to know there is no right or wrong way to grieve; I want you to know that the pain will not last forever; I want you to know that you will find peace. If this book has not helped you—and if this book *has* helped you, too—please consider utilizing some of the resources provided. Grief is always hard, there is no hack to fast-forward through this experience, but you don't have to bear the load alone.

Acknowledgements

This book could not be complete without first thanking several people. Thank you, first and foremost, to my mom and sister for a whole plethora of different things: thank you for dealing with me, thank you for encouraging me and this book, thank you for reading these poems even though reliving our loss is difficult. Thank you for being you, thank you for being safe people to cry to, and I'm sorry for making you cry, too, in the process. I love you both so very much.

Thank you also, Aunt Eydie and Uncle Jerry, for your unending support through every project I undertake, and thank you for pulling us into your immediate family, for being our support system, no questions asked. Thank you for making sure we were never alone.

Thank you, Hunter, for reading everything I write, for being so invested in the creation of this collection, and for helping me unpack all the overwhelming and not-so-pleasant feelings that accompany this kind of project. I don't think I would have actually done this if I didn't feel like I had to live up to your unconditional faith in me.

And thank you, of course, to Mary and my former colleagues at the Long Island University Post Writing Center for encouraging freewriting and creative writing and for pushing me to carve out time for creative writing like this. So many of these pieces were born of our Writing Wednesdays or written to share in our weekly staff meetings. I have so much appreciation for you all.

Gina Mingoia is a professor of English at St. Joseph's University, New York and a PhD student at the State University of New York at Stony Brook.

Jacqueline Mingoia, the designer of this cover, is an artist, photographer, and graphic designer. She lives in New York with her fiancé and an abundance of plants.

About Lightning Tower Press

Sal Mingoia always urged his two daughters to do what they love: to make time for the hobbies they love, to choose careers they love, and to live lives they love. Avid readers, his daughters Samantha and Gina always made time to read. When Gina chose to pursue a career in writing (because she loves it), she and Samantha realized just how difficult it is to break into the writing world. Many publishers require literary agents, making it difficult for low-income writers to have their works considered for publication, and, upon publication, many publishers demand a large portion of proceeds from the book sales. This makes it incredibly difficult for writers to be writers. So, after years of complaining about publisher gatekeeping, Samantha and Gina decided to simply start their own company: Lightning Tower Press. Lightning Tower Press, in honor of Sal Mingoia, is dedicated to helping writers do what they love.